ALAN MACFARLANE was b\.   ... ~..uung, India, in 1941 and educated at the Dragon School, Sedbergh School, Oxford and London Universities. He is the author of over twenty published books, including *The Origins of English Individualism* (1978) and *Letters to Lily: On How the World Works* (2005). He has worked in England, Nepal, Japan and China as both an historian and anthropologist.

He was elected to the British Academy in 1986 and is now Emeritus Professor of Anthropology at the University of Cambridge and a Life Fellow of King's College, Cambridge.

How To Discover The World

The World

Reflections for Rosa

ALAN MACFARLANE

CAM RIVERS
PUBLISHING

2018

First published in 2017
Second edition published in 2018 by

Cam Rivers Publishing Ltd
5 Canterbury Close
Cambridge CB4 3QQ

www.cambridgerivers.com
press@cambridgerivers.com

Author: Alan Macfarlane
Series Editor: Zilan Wang
Editor: Sarah Harrison
Marketing Manager: James O'Sullivan
Typesetting and cover design: Jaimie Norman

The Kaifeng Foundation generously supports the publishing of this book

For Rosa Blakely, with my love.

Alan Macfarlane, 2017

Contents

ONE

Why I Am Writing to You

'Make things as simple as possible—but not simpler'
'It is better to be roughly right than precisely wrong'
'The only source of knowledge is experience'
'It is a miracle that curiosity survives formal education'

—ALBERT EINSTEIN

D EAR ROSA,

I wrote a series of *Letters to Lily* to your sister. As these developed over the years they were turned into a survey and summary of what I have found out about the world over the last forty years. They are the nearest I can get to explaining what I think are the underlying tendencies and traps which surround us. By writing my thoughts down in a simple form I hoped to provide some guidance in this chaotic world, showing that behind the turbulence there are some patterns. These *Letters* described the results, the findings, the mechanisms of 'How the World Works.'

In the reflections for you, Rosa, I want to get down on paper a summary of what I have found out, through long experience, are the best ways to discover interesting things, some of the tools of thought.

This is a subject which has long interested me and I have written a great deal about it, much of it unpublished, and the rest in technical and academic pieces some of which are on my web-site. Now seems a good time to bring all this together in a clearer and simpler form, just as I did for Lily.

In the early seventeenth century one of the most brilliant thinkers of all time, Renée Descartes, reputedly retired into a large oven, a room for cooking bread, in Holland. Warm and cut off from the world he spent a few weeks writing a *Discourse on Method*. This explained that by following certain very simple methods, even people of quite average intelligence could solve really complex problems. Descartes said that he was such a person and that by the help of these simple techniques he had managed to make discoveries and solve problems which, without these methods, he could not possibly have done.

Descartes outlined his four methodological rules as follows. 'The first rule was to accept as true nothing that I did not know to be evidently so...' This is the method of doubt. Question everything, build your logic on a firmly established foundation. The second 'was to divide each difficulty I should examine into as many parts as possible, and as would be required the better to solve it.' The third rule 'was to conduct my thoughts in an orderly fashion, starting with what was simplest and easiest to know, and rising little by little to the knowledge of the most complex, even supposing an order where there is no natural precedence among the objects of knowledge.' His fourth rule was 'to make so complete an enumeration of the links in an argument, and to pass them all so thoroughly under review, that I could be sure I had missed nothing.'

Descartes reminds me of a mountaineering instructor. He had scaled difficult mountains, but pointed out that he could not have done so without certain mental equipment. However talented, intelligent and curious we are, we will never climb among the higher peaks unless we have the equivalent of good spiked shoes, warm clothing, a good tent, strong ropes. What Descartes was trying to explain was what worked for him, in the hope that it would also be useful for others. He was modest about his aims, writing 'Thus, my present design is not to teach the method which each one is bound to employ for the proper conduct of his reason, but only to show how I have conducted mine.' This is what I shall try to do for you, Rosa.

In order to puzzle out how the world around us works, to come up with creative solutions and learn new things, is a kind of detective work. We are flooded with sensations and faced with mysteries. In many disciplines, and these include biology, history, sociology, anthropology, a more useful method than that suggested by Descartes is to become a detective. Descartes' method is fine for mathematics and physics, where you start with some known axioms and rules and then proceed, through heavily controlled experiments, to discover unknown things. But much of our lives is different. Events have happened (history) or are happening (social sciences) and we try to understand them. This is much closer to the work of detectives.

The greatest detectives like Dupin and Sherlock Holmes solved crimes which ordinary people of equal intelligence could not solve. They did so through the application of certain methods which they had found worked. In the stories told about them, we not only see their results, but learn how they work. Indeed, much of the pleasure of reading these books lies in the way in which a master detective explains to an amazed accomplice (for example Watson), and thereby the reader, how he works. He is in a way a master who is instructing his apprentice in the 'mysteries' of his craft.

This is precisely what much of my life has been about. I am a 'Master of Arts', a sort of magician or detective who is paid not only to discover new things and write them down but also to pass on my craft to my students. Over the last forty years I have taken on 'apprentices', whether undergraduates or graduates at Cambridge University and tried to teach them about the *tools of thought*, ways of approaching problems, a far more useful thing than the content. Give people a fishing rod and let them catch their own fish, rather than handing out the fish.

Yet while all teachers try to pass on techniques all the time, we seldom explicitly think about what we are doing and what these tools are. There are, of course, numerous books written by teachers on how to write a thesis or essay or other piece of work. Yet it is noticeable that they are not usually written by those who are simultaneously engaged at the frontiers of knowledge. It is often an accident, such as Descartes wanting warmth in a cold winter's exile, or the historian Marc Bloch in a prisoner of war camp writing the *Craft of the Historian* because he was cut off from his actual work, that leads to the few reflections by those who have actually used the tools and become masters in their field. Usually, given the excitement of discovery, people are too busy doing research to have time to spend precious time teaching *others* how to discover.

* * *

When I was setting out to write the *Letters to Lily* I faced a particularly deep problem, which also applies here. There was no point in writing those *Letters* if there was nothing to report. In other words, if there are no patterns or tendencies or principles in human affairs, no tides in the affairs of men, then the *Letters* are pointless. And since quite a lot of intelligent men (and women) had come to the conclusion that there are no patterns, what could I tell Lily? After much thought I came to the conclusion that while there are no laws, there are tendencies, probabilities, likelihoods. The *Letters* explain what they are.

The same applies with the tools or methods of thought. In mathematics, music and perhaps mountaineering (certainly in fishing or film-making, which I know better) there are certain useful methods or tools. Of course these tools guarantee nothing. The best fisherman may catch nothing on a particular day, the best poet writing nothing of worth for a year, the best mathematician fail to solve a problem for ten years. On the other hand, the methods or tools put people in a position where they *may* achieve their goal. Without the tools, the job is impossible. They create the pre-conditions for success. As the saying is, 'Nature favours the prepared mind.' Perhaps the mountain, equation, painting, poem will be climbed, solved, created.

Is this also the case in the wide area which might be called the humanities and social sciences? Are there techniques and methods, approaches which I have learnt and then used and seem to have helped me and are worth passing on to others? And are these things which, if I tell you about, also may help you to figure out the world?

On the face of it, it seems likely. In every branch of our life we consult people and books about how to do things, whether it is learning to cook, garden, drive, use a computer or many other skills. We learn how to play the piano, paint, photograph, make films and other creative activities. We learn languages, mathematics and how to write. All these are transmissible skills, a mixture of example and practice. These *Letters* could be seen as a sort of manual on how to think and communicate productively.

The moment I write that sentence 'to think and communicate productively', the difficulty of the task re-emerges. Almost all the skills I have talked about above are subsidiary skills, like fishing, gardening or even mathematics. What I shall be writing to you about is the central one that lies behind them all, namely how to think creatively at a high level and to discover and solve really exciting problems.

This sounds a bit like the work of people like Edward de Bono on *Lateral Thinking*, and no doubt it is. But this is not primarily a manual on effective thinking, though it does deal with that. It is rather a set of reflections on what I have learnt, passing on what I think is the essence of how I actually work.

TWO

Ask Absurb Questions

'Unless an idea starts off as absurd, there is no chance for it'

'To know is nothing at all; to imagine is everything'

'It is the theory which decides what we can observe'

'The normal adult never bothers his head about space-time problems. Everything there is to be thought about, in his opinion, has already been done in early childhood. I, on the contrary, developed so slowly that I began to wonder about space and time when I was already grown up. In consequence I probed deeper into the problem than an ordinary child would have done'

—ALBERT EINSTEIN

D EAR ROSA,

One of the most important questions concerns the choice of what we should investigate. To a certain extent this question was taken out of the hands of the great detectives upon whom I shall model my advice. People presented themselves with puzzles and riddles and then they were investigated. For most of us, however, deciding what questions to ask is one of the most difficult things.

Many people think that solving a puzzle, finding the answers, is the hard part. It is indeed hard, but often not as hard or as important as finding the question. The Chinese say that a journey of a thousand miles starts with one step. But in which direction should we step? Often we don't know the goal, so how can we set out?

Others point out that if we pose a question badly, then we shall never get any interesting or convincing answers. Others suggest that almost inevitably we will ask the same questions as everyone else – and so just repeat their answers. As Einstein commented, by the age of 18 we are surrounded by 'common sense', which is really the accumulation of everyone's prejudices.

What I am hoping to provide for you is a set of tools to escape from the 'fly bottle', to challenge the orthodoxy, to think new and original thoughts. Yet how is that possible when we do not know what is unknown, we do not know what are interesting questions, we do not, in effect, know what questions we should ask?

The logical thing would be to ask safe, sensible, logical, questions, questions to which we know there must be a chance of finding an answer. We know from our experience that if we ask our parents or friends large and ambitious questions, they are likely to turn away and say that it would take too long to explain, no-one knows the answers and so on. So we are discouraged and tend to stick to safer, answerable questions. The sort of questions we asked as a child – what is the meaning of life, why do people have to die, what is God really like, why is there so much pain, in other words the questions I have tried to answer for your sister Lily – are too large and our elders brush them aside.

It is not a bad thing to answer smaller questions and to test out our skills in answering them, just as in sports or games or art we try out relatively easy moves to gain practice. Yet the important thing is to realize that this is just a start. Again and again those who have made major contributions and thought deeply have emphasized how we should ask large, apparently crazy, questions. There are many quotations to the effect that unless we ask impertinent questions, we will never get pertinent answers.

Of course many of the crazier questions or strange hypotheses are off the mark, unanswerable, ridiculous. Yet unless we attempt them, we shall be stuck in the middle ground of the safe, but generally a bit boring. Unless we let our imagination and intuition have free play, there is no chance that we will make unusual, unanticipated, hitherto unknown, connections.

The more interesting questions have two components built into them. They ask a question, but in the question there is probably also a conjecture or implicit guess at an answer. The great difficulty is that there is no rational or logical method which suggests how to formulate these questions and conjectures. Once made, we can proceed quite logically to try to test them. But the initial question is a guess. As the great French mathematician Poincaré put it 'Guessing before demonstrating that is how all science proceeds.' The common idea that many of us have that we start with an experiment, which generates some ideas, is wrong. As Einstein suggested, experiment are the results, not the origins, of intuitions.

We are helped by the fact that in any area of thought there is usually a half-recognized set of assumptions, knowledge and conventional questions which provides a person with lots of sub-questions to pursue. This is a world-view which holds sway at a point in history covering a number of disciplines. This world view sets the task for those who are trying to decide what to ask.

So if we look at any form of art or science we find that most people busily fill in the gaps of knowledge, they work within a set of possible thoughts.

Most knowledge producers are like a team of bridge-builders. The task of Renaissance or Impressionist painters, of classical or romantic poets, of evolutionary or functional sociologists, is broadly established for them. There is a wide river to be crossed. Certain predecessors have built a light archway across. The majority of people are busy putting in the supports, painting and strengthening the structure.

In such a situation the questions are roughly suggested for us. Our teachers will set them in our essays and in our exams and when we come to do our research we will merely go into them in more depth. I have lived surrounded by such world views (though they are largely invisible to us) and relied on them as automatic question-setting mechanisms throughout my life.

When I was studying history in Oxford a new theory was emerging, which shifted the emphasis from the political to the social and the economic, from the national to the local. The questions had largely been laid out by a previous generation of sociologists and anthropologists, or by French historians. My job was to take these questions and to find the evidence and the answers. So I took the functional questions about witchcraft developed by anthropologists and applied them to sixteenth and seventeenth century England. By doing this I came up with some new findings.

This is a good way to start. Take questions from one field and apply them in another, just as someone might take a crop like maize, which grew well in America and try it in China. Often it is especially fruitful in a new environment.

Usually there is an added bonus from such cross-fertilization. Asking what appears to be the same questions in another setting subtly alters the questions and gives new interpretations. The functionalist questions could not really address change, whereas asking them in an historical setting had to confront change. So the questions altered.

Or again, I remember my excitement when I realized that a central mechanism in witchcraft was the projection of blame onto the witch for causing the ambivalence which people felt. This was not something which had been noted in the classical literature on witches. It was a new idea in the world. It suddenly struck me from outside, as it were, though it lay so obviously on the surface of the documents.

So, working within a world view which both sets the questions and suggests roughly what will be acceptable answers, is what most of us do. It is helpful and necessary. There are limitations, however.

Even if we stay within the world view, we would like to show some independence, creativity, originality. Even if Wordsworth, Coleridge and Keats are all Romantic poets, they are very different. How can we both ask a common set of questions and accept a framework which determines what is a reasonable sort of answer, and at the same time break away enough to do something new and creative? These reflections will try to provide some hints on how I think this is done, based on my own experience.

There are degrees of novelty and originality. Most people come up with minor creative solutions; their houses, clothing, cooking, ideas are an original concoction within a fairly conventional frame. But there are those who become role models, at least in the West, because they changed a whole world view. The names are well known. In art, Bruneleschi, Leonardo, Durer, Rembrandt and many others; in music, Handel, Bach, Mozart; in science, Galileo, Newton, Darwin, Einstein among others. In philosophy and political philosophy, Descartes, Hobbes, Hume, Kant, Tocqueville and others. Very few of us can emulate them. Yet it does seem to me that we can learn from them.

The heavy pressure is towards conformity, towards limiting our ambition, towards accepting our weakness, towards trimming our questions. From very early on, a combination of peer, parental and school pressure, a realistic acceptance that we are not cleverer or more talented than those around us, pulls us back.

I have felt this all my life, recognizing that my sisters, mother and many of my friends have more natural gifts. I am not good at languages, music or art, mathematics and many other things. My memory is middling, my logical ability average, writing style mediocre. At school I scraped along. I have always identified with Einstein's remark that 'I have no special talents. I am only passionately curious.'

The one gift I had was self-belief and, following my school motto, I aimed at the stars. I wanted both to understand the world, and if possible, change it for the better. I never really did the latter, but have made some steps towards the former. Through hard work and the application of some of the mental tools which I shall explain to you. This was against the obstacles of dim, average, ability outlined above. How was this?

* * *

Well, a part of the answer lies in the ambition to ask crazy questions. Einstein recalls how as a child he asked those very large, child-like, questions we all ask, like 'What is the meaning of life, space, time' and so on. He was told to save them up for when he was grown up. He did so and went on asking them at an age when he had the tools to start to get answers. He discovered that 'wait until you are grown up' meant for most people that they stopped asking the questions. What they waited to find out was that the questions could not be answered. He refused to accept this.

This process of narrowing the questions is dissected by Wordsworth and Blake. The latter's aptly named 'Songs of Innocence and Experience' is about this loss of vision. These poets, like most great thinkers and artists, remained in some sense children. They still wanted to know the answers to big questions.

One of the great difficulties in searching for new things is that it requires abandoning some of the cosy strength of accepted world views, usually largely conveyed to us through education. We are heavily indoctrinated by the assembled conventional wisdom in a broad range of subjects. In order to progress through school and to university we have to learn and to a considerable extent accept and believe in the basic theory put to us in history, literature, the sciences.

These are all re-enforced by other streams of conventional thought from the television, magazines and papers, films, museums, and now of course by what is on the web. We are overwhelmed and flooded so that there are few recesses in the caves of our mind for any alternative views.

That is why many creative thinkers have found that one of the most extraordinary parts of their later life (as in *The Education of Henry Adams*) is to *unlearn* what they thought they knew and to start again. The *Letters* I am writing to you could be seen as an attempt to help you and I to examine what we know and to unlearn a great deal, to clear the decks, to use a common cliché.

This is why I shall devote a good deal of attention to things like the way to live, the virtues of travel and so on. The heavy burden of conventional wisdom is so great that it needs pretty drastic action to make us aware of it and to enable us to re-arrange our mental furniture. As Hobbes put it, if I read all the books which others read, I will think as others think.

Yet the difficulty is that *unless* we study enough of what others have done, we are in danger of re-inventing wheels, of becoming a voice in the wilderness, of becoming so cut off that we have no influence and probably little happiness. So a productive tension, 'in the world but not of the world', has to be maintained in our life and thought. These *Letters* will try to explain some of the ways you might go about this if you want to make the attempt.

* * *

One of the *Letters* I want to write to you Rosa is about intuition, about asking fruitful questions. It is often noticed of great scientists, for example Fred Sanger who is a Fellow of my College in Cambridge, the only living double Nobel laureate, that, like wine tasters or bloodhounds, they have a 'nose.' They have a kind of implicit skill at finding out what are really major areas to concentrate their attention upon.

Although some of this is based on deep knowledge and a lot of it on experience of what works, are there any things which we can say about acquiring this 'nose'? How does one train it, what tips can we have about it? Here are just a few scattered thoughts as they occur to me, which will need to be put into order, fleshed out in more detail.

One is that we should not be put off by early disappointments. Often people give up too son. They ask a fascinating question which is just about to lead somewhere. For a while they do not seem to get anywhere and give up just before they find the treasure. I tried to teach you this skill when we did the endless treasure hunts in our house and garden when you were young.

Another tip is that we should not be put off in the early stages by logical criticisms. The early stages of any really worthwhile endeavour consist of imagining impossible connections, making crazy, half right, half wrong, guesses. Any sane friend can easily destroy these thoughts in their infancy. So I have learnt not to discuss my early hunches with your granny Sarah, and she has learnt to restrain her curiosity because of this danger. Too much rational argument can destroy the dreams. The infant ideas must be allowed to grow for a while until they are stronger.

Most dangerous of all, I suppose, are our own self-doubts and self-criticisms. Many thinkers have been systematically trained to destroy ideas, their own as well as others. It is very difficult to be charitable to our own half-baked (almost literally) thoughts. Even as I write this Letter, I keep thinking of how facile, obvious, rather boring, illogical it all is. Never mind – get the outrageous or boring things down and then see if there is something there.

I do expect, however, that there will be a good deal to say about encouraging intuition in deciding what the questions are. For instance, there is the whole realm of what causes wonder and curiosity in the first place. What makes us ask questions?

This is something which the philosopher Adam Smith spent much time thinking about and made some very good observations on. Or again, there is the need to separate the first large questions, of the 'how does the world work' level, from the middle-level questions like 'are humans naturally violent', to the more specific, like 'what does one mean by violence?' or 'can we describe football as violent.' There are clearly different levels of questions.

Another area concerns who the questions are for. Are they to satisfy our own curiosity, that of our friends and family, our students, the world, the present, the future? It is like the common advice given to writers to think carefully about their audience. In a sense we need to ask ourselves 'Why are we asking?' 'Who cares?' 'So what?'

Another area is about the relationship between questions and conjectures. Many questions have built into them a guess or hypothesis about a possible answer. Columbus asked himself whether it would be possible to travel westwards and find a route to China – and guessed that it would. So he set out. If he'd asked the question and conjectured that it was impossible, he would not have started. The question and the conjecture are intimately linked. 'Is the moon made of cheese? Almost certainly not.' A boring question and likely answer. 'Is there intelligent life in space? Perhaps.' An exciting question and an uncertain answer.

So there is the fruitful question, the half-plausible conjecture to test, and finally there is the evidence – the chance of proving the conjecture right or wrong. Here is where all the 'science' bit comes in—the experimentation, the looking for evidence and data. One large thing to consider here is how much and what evidence is enough.

The larger the question and the more important it is, the less likely the evidence will be conclusive, or even available. If people ask, 'Is there a God?' or 'Do humans have souls? Or 'How will the world end?', they find no convincing answers and a great deal of dubious speculation based on hazy sightings of partial evidence. If they ask, 'which is the shortest route by road from A to B', they are likely to get very precise information. If they ask, will global warming make England hotter or colder in fifty years, the authorities cannot answer. If they ask 'will it rain here tomorrow', they may get an answer with a higher than random chance of being correct.

Some people take this as a warning not to ask the large questions. They feel we should limit our seeking to those areas where there is plenty of evidence which will definitely prove the case one way or another. Some historians argue that their skill lies in knowing the sources well enough to know what would be fruitful questions. There is no point, for instance, in asking what ordinary people in the middle ages dreamt about since there is scarcely any evidence existing to answer the question.

There is something in this, but it has the danger of becoming a circular and self-fulfilling prophecy. It is true that many inexperienced researchers ask interesting but ultimately frustrating questions to which there can never be an answer. It is disastrous for them if they set out for four years of research believing they will find an answer. On the other hand there is a rather magical tendency for questions to generate new evidence, just as my thyme plant seems to generate the soil upon which it flourishes on our stone courtyard.

I remember attending a seminar at the Institute of Historical Research in about 1967 when a leading historian of Tudor England proclaimed that sixteenth century historical studies were finished, dead, because we had run out of materials. Everything had been sifted through, all possible questions asked. The century had been mined out.

Yet this was at the very point when the vast materials in local archives were just becoming available and a whole new set of questions were askable. People very frequently do not open doors because they are convinced that there is nothing behind them.

* * *

Another difficulty in the asking of interesting questions is what we might call the boundary, or division of labour, problem. As knowledge progresses it inevitably tends to get divided up. In order to succeed, people are trained as specialists. At one time someone can ask about big things, for little is known. 'Renaissance man' is a short-hand for this, people like Montaigne, Leonardo da Vinci, Francis Bacon, Montesquieu, Adam Smith span almost all of human knowledge. But now we have to be specialists, a part of a team. A scientist is an expert on one gene, a historian on one aspect of one country in one century, a literary critic on one author. Pushed outside their speciality they no longer feel at ease.

It is not difficult to see why this should happen and indeed it is necessary. It is prudent and helpful to have a specialization, to be *the* world authority on something or other, however small. Detailed, microscopic, 'world in a grain of sand', work is essential.

The difficulty is that, as with animals that become trapped by over-specializing in a micro-habitat, it is very easy to become so cramped and tunnel-visioned that not only can we not ask large and interesting questions, but even our micro-study becomes lop-sided. I agree with Einstein that it is better to get things 'roughly right rather than precisely wrong.'

Most of us have met people who have concentrated so much on something that they have lost a sense of proportion. They can no longer see the thing itself clearly. Most things only have a meaning in context and only by setting them in a wider frame can we begin to ask interesting questions about them.

It is a considerable problem. In order to be a good historian, chemist, biologist or whatever, we have to specialize. Yet most of the interesting questions not only force us out of our specialisms within these disciplines, they usually require us to traspass on other people's territory. I have often found this.

Yet this is an essential part of research. As the historian Lord Acton wrote, 'study problems and not periods.' We have to follow the question beyond its originally defined boundaries. But what if we broaden this saying to 'study problems, not disciplines'? A whole new set of difficulties emerge.

There is a further complication, which could be introduced by another version: 'study problems, not places.' I was trained to study the history of England, but early knew that 'He little of England knows who only England knows.' The insular, comforting, depth of local study available to people in the 1960s has gone in the frequent calls to 'global' this and that. A moment's thought will make us aware that interesting questions will not halt at national borders, any more than they will at the start and end of a century or the edge of a discipline.

Yet there is the same problem of trespassing. It is bad enough for a seventeenth century historian of England to pronounce on nineteenth century English history. Even worse if she starts to find that as an economic historian she has to trespass on the fields of medicine or chemistry. But what if her problem requires her to say things about whole civilizations whose language, history and culture she knows nothing about? Surely, this path will quickly lead to out of date, second-hand and shallow work?

So there are numerous questions about question asking. How large, how detailed, how crazy, how sensible, how confined to possible data, how are they arrived at, how can experience give a 'nose'? Yet it is the first and most important stage, and always subject to the fact that the questions will alter. Explorations is ultimately about finding the questions, not the answers.

THREE

Guess Before Demonstrating

'Anyone who has never made a mistake has never tried anything new'
'The only really valuable thing is intuition'
'How do I work? I grope'
'The formulation of a problem is often more essential than its solution,
which may be merely a matter of mathematical or experimental skill'

—ALBERT EINSTEIN

D EAR ROSA,

Let's look at the next stage in thinking about problems. We have a question or set of questions in our mind. What next?

What is a guess or conjecture? Why is it important in research and how do we make fruitful guesses? We can start with the use of the word conjecture by the philosopher Dugald Stewart. Writing of the methods of his predecessors David Hume and Adam Smith and others he described them as developing a fruitful system of 'conjectural history.' What he meant in modern language was that out of their deep experience of the world, and from the surviving historical materials, they were able to build up a sketch or simplified set of inter-connected features (a 'model') of what *probably* happened over long periods in the past.

There are several features of a conjecture. Firstly it is based on a mixture of experience, parallels and analogies, some existing evidence. Yet it is also as yet a guess, a surmise, unproven, and perhaps unprovable for want of further evidence. It is a 'just so' story which gives a believable or plausible framework to account for what the author currently knows. It is provisional, refutable, subject to alteration. It is often complex. That is to say, it is not usually just a single guess, for instance that a certain event led to another, but a whole story or interlinked model accounting for a large subject. It is often a narrative of some kind.

Therefore it is a kind of imagined history, a 'most likely' explanation, which gives satisfaction in the present state of knowledge. Conjectures can be on various scales, more or less firm, more or less complex, based on more or less evidence, more or less ambitious.

Of course, from one point of view, most of our life is based on conjectures, that is mental models of what is likely to be the case, but for which we have insufficient evidence as yet to be certain. Travelling is based on endless conjectures about the behaviour of traffic, the nature of the road, the nature of the destination. We travel in hope and expectation on the basis of guesswork. Often we are roughly right, sometimes disappointed, sometimes amazed that the actuality differs greatly from our conjecture.

Conjectures are thought experiments. They should draw on all that we have learnt about the world so that the conjectures of experienced persons will often be more accurate. They should include a first approximation for all the relevant data on the subject in hand. Yet they are ultimately created away from the world, in the study, at the desk, in conversation.

The whole realm of art and literature is in a way a giant set of conjectures. A novel by Dickens or Jane Austen is a set of conjectures, based on experience, as to how people would behave under certain conditions. It cannot easily be proved wrong, but may well seem implausible and unconvincing. Conjectures tend to be constantly in need of adjustment. They are like rough drafts, of a painting, chapter of a book, a television documentary. They start off fairly simple and with obvious flaws; inaccuracies, false assumption, illogicalities. These begin to emerge as they are placed against the evidence. So they are constantly modified, hopefully improved, until the conjecture turns into the final description or asserted truth.

Part of the difficulty here is that we cannot separate conjectures off from other parts of the discovery process. The original question we are asking is a backward reflection, as it were, of the conjecture. We often start with a conjecture, for example 'glass changed the world', and this then generates some questions – how did it do so, why did it do so in some parts of the world and not others?

Conjectures also cast a forward light, determining where we look for evidence for their confirmation or refutation. A good conjecture can be looked on as a net. The size of its meshes will determine what fish are caught, or let to swim through (the fish being so-called 'facts'). If the conjectures are too specific, the net will become clogged with an over-abundance of trivial facts. If the conjecture is too vague, almost everything will swim through and perhaps only a few banal and unexciting platitudes will be captured.

There is also the question of what if the net breaks. Here the correcting or adapting feature of conjectures comes in. There is a considerable investment in building up a working model or set of hunches about what we expect to find. On the other hand, one attraction of conjectures is that being a sort of blueprint or explicit plan, worked out on a 'drawing board', it *should* not be too much effort to 'go back to the drawing board' as the cliché puts it. In other words, to make a drastic re-drawing, or even to throw away the original and start again.

In many ways the adaptation of the conjectural model is far less painful than re-arranging the evidence. The evidence is like the stones, bricks and beams of the building. They have a solidity, weight and resistance to change. Once they are in place, to move one may entail a huge effort. But conjectures are mental constructs and though we become wedded to them, they should be easier to modify.

* * *

One odd thing about conjectures is that their fruitfulness does not mainly lie in their final accuracy. Many of the most amazing findings have been made on the basis of wildly inaccurate conjectures – Columbus and America being a notable example (and many in medicine no doubt). What they provide above all is a preliminary, confidence-inducing, map. Without conjectures we would not start out on the journey. So the more ambitious and exciting the conjecture, the more likely it is to lead somewhere interesting.

If we think of conjectures as setting goals, things to aim for, then it is obvious that if they are very humdrum and limited, little will be achieved. Many great scientists have spoken of the need for wild, crazy, mad conjectures.

This is linked to something else. If we think of finding out exciting new things as like gold mining, then we find ourselves surrounded by masses of other equally energetic and intelligent prospectors, many of them much more experienced. If we follow the logical, sensible, careful rules of prospecting, we will hunt where many have hunted before us and there is very little chance of finding something new. So we should forget the sensible and the rules and set out on our own way.

This is probably why most major discoveries seem to be a combination of a 'prepared mind', that is someone like Fleming who has a set of questions or even conjectures, and complete accident – the dirty petrie dish which led to penicillin being discovered. The conjectures can be worked out fairly rationally, and they should be as ambitious, and perhaps counter-intuitive, as possible. But in the end they cannot be guaranteed to generate anything magnificent.

The fish swim according to laws which we do not understand. We lay the nets and traps, but in the end it is up to the gods as to what we find in the morning. Conjectures are the tools, the nets, the bows, the maps, yet the best of tools will not necessarily produce anything worthwhile.

There is obviously a lot to be said about how to formulate good conjectures. If they are guesses, how best to put ourselves in a position to guess? Here there is another odd paradox, which reverts back to the fact that all the logical prospecting will already have been tried.

* * *

While it is possible to sit at our desk and draw up plans, maps, conjectural nets to catch the fish, usually the really valuable conjectures occur in apparently idle moments.

There are numerous stories from the bath moment of 'Eureka', through Einstein's waking vision, through Poincaré and others, which illustrate this. It is very often on walks, listening to music, on a journey, or in a moment between sleep and waking.

The nearest I can at present get to guessing why this should be is that in order to try something new, the mind has to perform an incredibly complex and not strictly logical operation. It has to leap across ruts and conventional categories, it has to look in unlikely places.

It is like hunting for something that has been lost. After looking in the obvious places and finding nothing, it is best to store the lost thing in our mind and go on to other things. Usually, accidentally, wrongly classified, it will be bumped into again and recognized.

Much research is like this. We know from the conjectural frame the rough shape of what we are looking for, but not exactly where or even what it is. The skill, as in Fleming's case, or that in the discovery of 'splitting the atom', is to recognize it when we see it, whereas most people just pass over it as not interesting.

* * *

One danger arising from the interplay between the conjectures (the net) and the 'facts' (the fish) is that we will construct the evidence to support our conjecture. This is not necessarily deliberate cheating, but rather that it is in the nature of nets and conjectures to make certain things invisible (the fish that swim through) and others are seen or caught.

We are surrounded by a mass of sensations and see many

things which we do not notice. There is a danger of self-confirming hypotheses or prophecies. We expect a connection, we find the evidence to support it. We proclaim the finding. This will take us into a whole area of how we turn conjectures into more or less reliable knowledge, how we refute arguments.

For the moment, however, what I want to point out is that the idea that we approach a problem with an empty and objective mind and just 'look at the evidence' and then form our theories is impossibly naïve. Of course it should be our goal to avoid blind ideology or such strong conjectures that we cannot see important facts or crush them when they get in the way of our beliefs. Most people are horrified by the manipulation that extreme communism and other religions force on their adherents. That end of research where the political or religious conjecture is more important than the honest attempt to discover the world as it is, should be avoided.

To go in with too strong a framework, and particularly if it has been taken over largely unexamined from someone else is unfortunate. An iron-chain net, for instance strong communist or fascist beliefs, will only catch (and mutilate) a few fish. The danger here, of course, is that the researcher has beliefs first and then looks for facts to buttress those beliefs. A 'buttress' is only to stablilize a building. What if the building is unstable and should be re-built?

The idea that, for example, we can go into a library, archive, or village and 'just look' at 'the facts' without any prejudices or pre-conceived sorting and filtering framework is clearly wrong. The art is to get the balance right. We have to arrive with some hypotheses or conjectures and expectations, otherwise we will find nothing. All discovery is a matter of finding the deviations from our expectations. We only notice differences. If we have no expectations, everything will strike us as equally interesting, or uninteresting. There is no separating mechanism.

* * *

Another difficulty has increasingly emerged in relation to discussions of what is sometimes called 'objectivity' and 'subjectivity.' If we reject the idea of 'purely objective', 'facts without hypotheses', working from the facts to the theories (inductivist), calling them all, as many do, 'naïve empiricism', it looks as if we may be faced with a wholly relativist alternative. We may seem to be in a situation where all facts are 'constructed' by the observer's ideology. It seems attractive to argue that our conjectures are deeply influenced by our ideologies and our ideologies by our class, gender, colonial, educational or whatever position.

Taking this position, we could argue that only women can study women's history, only people in India can study Indian society and so on. If we take the logic on, then only a middle class Indian woman from Bangalore can understand middle-class women from Bangalore, and then only those of her own age and educational background.

This recent loss of confidence can lead into a morass of reflexive, 'navel' or mirror gazing, self-analysis and doubt which leaves the researcher paralysed and unable to proceed. Who am I to say such a thing? What right have I to have theories or even investigate this? Am I not just constructing stories to suit my prejudices?

The refutation of this comes from our daily experience. We

know that important things have been discovered in the past, that even if all science is approximation (including the laws of physics), that many technologies do work. We know that there is a solid world outside our brains, made of things which hurt us if we bump into them.

We know that although we make our conjectures and plans based on faulty, colonialized, gendered, class-based, prejudices, we often seem to get things roughly right. Humans are much more intelligent and detached from their narrow ideologies in practice than would seem to be likely if we judged them from their background. Almost anybody can do anything if encouraged. Even the highest science, as Einstein asserted, is just elevated common sense.

There is another practical refutation. We have to make guesses, and to believe in them, in order to lead orderly lives. A railway, school or university timetable is a complex conjecture based on probabilities. Sending a rocket to the moon is based on many conjectures. All planning for the future is based on guesses, however flawed.

Likewise all understanding of the past is ultimately conjectural, a matter of probabilities. We cannot know for certain what went through the mind of Oliver Cromwell, Napoleon or Genghis Khan. We cannot know for certain what tipped a battle in one direction, or led to a great insight or painting. We can only construct more or less confining conjectural pictures. Likewise in legal cases, the jury is faced with a set of conjectures after the fact and they have to decide which is the most likely or 'reasonable.'

So, as with all knowledge, we are not dealing with binary choices, true or false, but rather things which are more fruitful, exciting, elegant, beautiful, more convincing, inclusive, always more or less along a continuum. One criterion for judging the power of a conjecture is its complexity or simplicity. As the medieval philosopher Ockham argued with his logical 'razor', if there are two explanations which work equally well, choose the simpler. The more that can be explained by the least words or symbols, the better; 'the survival of the fittest', 'all power tends to corrupt', '$e=mc^2$.' Nature abhors verbosity or prolixity, or, as Thoreau would say, 'simplify, simplify.'

Related to this is the lever principle. That is to say, not only do we judge the value of a lever by its simplicity of operation, but also by the amount it can lift. A complex conjecture which leads to little understanding – which is the charge made against much modern 'structuralist' and 'post-modern' writing – is unhelpful. A simple conjecture which opens up a world, which is what many find in the work of great writers such as Shakespeare or Orwell, changes everything. If it is true that man cannot stand too much reality, it is also true that she cannot stand too much complexity.

This is the nature of models, which is really what conjectures are. They simplify, reducing things to their essentials and thus diminishing the size and scale, without losing the interconnections. In building conjectures, we build models.

Yet while we aim for final simplicity in the conjectures, the usual experience is of a three-fold process. We start with simplicity and then in the light of experience and testing, the conjecture gets more and more complicated. Then, hopefully, as we reach deeper, it becomes simpler again. Many painters, poets, writers and scientists have experienced this.

Start with a simple idea or conjecture – for example that it might be an interesting idea to get down all my thoughts on how to discover the world as a set of letters to you, Rosa. Then let numerous conjectures and complexities and difficulties and opportunities emerge which lead to a tangled, over-elaborate and verbose expression of the conjectures. Then, hopefully, simplify down to the core shape.

There are many analogies. A sculptor starts with a model in her head and a block of stone and gradually reduces. A gold prospector goes to a place and refines and refines until only the gold is left. Conjectures and their evolution are like that.

* * *

What else can be said about conjectures? It is advisable to operate at several levels simultaneously. Have safe bets and outsider ones, as in racing or the stock exchange. Just to take extreme risks on outsiders is probably suicidal unless we are very rich in time and resources. Yet just to bet on the favourites is not only boring but unlikely to achieve much.

So you should make grand, amazing, improbable, impossible conjectures, but keep them to yourself and only announce them when a reasonable amount of evidence is there. Otherwise you will get the reputation for being slightly crazy. Have some middling, amusing, unlikely, but intriguing conjectures just to try out on people. And then have some worthy, sensible, logical conjectures to provide the bread and butter, what is sometimes called 'normal science.'

It is good to keep modifying and altering the conjectures. One way to do this with a plan or map. Personally I make plans or maps of where I think I am proceeding with a project quite frequently – every few months. At the fever point of creativity I have found that the plans have altered drastically every day or two. Also there may be some months of stability when not much changes.

There is, of course, a strong resistance to making these plans and conjectures. It seems somehow to take away from the objectivity of research if we put down in black and white what we expect to find in advance. It also seems premature to make a grand conjecture or plan even after we have gathered a huge amount of material.

These difficulties can usually be overcome if we just head the plan 'First Plan, Very Provisional, to be altered completely' or some such. The plans are just snap-shots, cross-sections of where we think we are. They help to order materials and give direction, but they have no finality and little predictive power. Looking back over the plans of both myself and my students, the final book or thesis usually has its kernel in the early plans, but almost everything has been changed. Of necessity it is vague, as vague as most of our plans when we go on a holiday or even a long car journey. We sketch out a few points on the way, but fill in the details as we go along, and may even alter the route entirely depending on what we come across.

This is the final point I shall make about conjectures here. They must be flexible and provisional, guides to thought and action, but not fossilized. They are thought experiments, with a lot of thought but little experiment. Almost certainly the more exciting, wild and potentially explosive they are, the more they will take us into territory which will show that they need serious modification. Conjectures which stick close to common sense and to what is already known will probably need little modification. They are models based on a great deal of data and there is a more or less 1:1 relationship with what they represent.

Yet a crazy hypothesis, that men are descended from monkeys, that time and space are related, that the earth goes round the sun, that we can sail west to China, usually lead to huge contra evidence which needs modifications and re-analysis.

* * *

Difficult voyages, based on a wild surmise, lead inevitably to disappointments and hardships. They have probably already been attempted by others who have become dispirited, despaired and given up. By definition, the gratifications and discoveries are deferred; the oceans are wide and no land is sighted for a long time. The conjectures thus become a sort of faith, a belief, a hope and confidence to be held in times of deadness and despair. Cling onto them as long as you can. Maybe keep the smaller ones alongside to provide some income or benefits. But do not be put off too soon.

There are innumerable stories of important break-throughs which were nearly made, but the person gave up just too soon. Perhaps she walked past the door without knowing, perhaps she pushed but not hard enough. Perhaps her eye swept over something but was too tired or too abstracted to see it. Perhaps the discovery was in such a minute detail (as I shall explain) that she ignored it. There are many reasons, and not least that people have to live, they have to give time to others, they have to feed their families.

Love, friendship, war, fear, almost everything we experience can knock us away from the pursuit of our conjectures. This is why I shall devote quite a lot of these *Letters* to what may seem incidental matters to do with organizing our life. Yet the way you organize your life has an enormous, if invisible, effect. The study of the great explorers and conjecturalists, from Captain Cook to Einstein, bears witness to the fact that personality and life style can have an immense effect on whether the conjectures are interesting and whether they lead to fruitful findings.

FOUR

Testing

'If we knew what we were doing it wouldn't be research'

'The important thing is not to stop questioning. Curiosity has its own reason for existing ... Never lose a holy curiosity.'

'No number of experts can prove me right. One experiment can prove me wrong.'

'If the facts don't fit the theory, change the facts'

—ALBERT EINSTEIN

D EAR ROSA,

It is at the point when you come to test a conjecture that the difference between the methods of the physical sciences (as Descartes described them) and the biological and social sciences (similar to detective work) become very obvious.

In essence, in physics, chemistry and similar disciplines, as I understand it, a person sets up a conjecture, for instance that A causes B, or B is caused by A and C. Then they do an experiment to test the conjecture. The experiment isolates the relevant things, the particles, elements, atoms or whatever, in a confined space and time (often in a 'laboratory') so that the investigator can see whether the conjecture appears to be right. In medical research there are special tests, double blind, placebos and others. Indeed in each of the 'hard' sciences there are particular features to the experiments.

The experiments are thought to 'prove' or 'disprove' a hypothesis. In fact, as in a court of law, they merely 'prove beyond all reasonable doubt', rather than absolutely. In other words they establish very high probabilities of the conjectured association, but can never absolutely prove that it is more than a coincidence.

The very high probability, or as we may call it, the high reliability, is guaranteed by the fact that we can force or 'torture' nature through the experiments. We can try to get results which will be replicated exactly if someone else repeats the experiment in an identical way. They establish that certain conditions are both necessary and sufficient to cause others. So we can be fairly sure that we have established laws of causation.

These methods are very powerful. If they could be used in the social sciences, there is no doubt that they would have been copied. But there are several reasons why they cannot. The first is ethical. There are severe criticisms of experimenting on animals. The experiments by the Germans and Japanese on human beings during the Second World War has caused outrage. With humans we can observe and do limited psychological and physical testing, but all is very limited. We can 'torture' nature, so we believe, but not our fellow men. So the whole extreme laboratory style is out of the question.

Furthermore, the sort of questions social scientists ask, as well as the nature of their object is very different. If they ask what causes wars, revolutions, the development of industrialism, witchcraft beliefs, it is obvious that they are questions which do not readily lend themselves to laboratory science. They have often already happened, and will never be repeated in an identical way. They are often of a size which precludes isolating in a test tube. It would take some test tube to fit in the current industrialization of China.

The typical model of social science problems is a crime. This is investigated by detectives (historians, sociologists), who try to find a plausible suspect and motive and then present the suspect to a court where he or she is tried before a judge. Arguments are put to try to persuade the judge that things did happen in a certain way, *beyond all reasonable doubt.*

It is assumed that humans behave in a certain way, the 'reasonable man (or woman)' hypothesis. It is argued that a certain reconstruction of a chain of events is the most plausible story to account for what we know happened. The judge (reader) then weighs the probabilities arising from the evidence and the arguments presented.

The crime itself is by definition unique and no attempt is made to repeat it. Yet it probably bears resemblances to other crimes and parts of it falls into recognizable patterns. As the anthropologist Clifford Geertz notes, 'history does not repeat itself, but it rhymes.' Looking for the rhyme gives some possibility of success.

If this distinction between the methods of the physical and social sciences is correct and the analogy with criminal investigation is true, it suggests that if we want to understand how best to move from conjecture to more reliable knowledge, it will be worth paying attention to the huge literature already existing in forensic science. In other words we should look at the methods of detective investigation and of legal evidence.

Basically what detectives do is to outline in considerable detail the methods of backwards reasoning, from effect to cause, which is the very same technique which social scientists, biologists and astronomers have to use. We cannot move forwards along a chain of *conjecture > experiment > conjecture 2 > experiment 2* in the way that Descartes advocates. In the social sciences, the phenomenon has happened or is happening and we are trying to understand it. The mystery is already present and we hope to solve it. So we need a series of techniques to make this possible. What these techniques will do is provide reasonably reliable knowledge to flesh out the conjectures. In a way the conjecture can be looked on as a very rough sketch for a painting, or a rough plan for a building or bridge. But the whole sketch or plan may be unworkable or unsatisfactory and it certainly lacks detail. Good detectives and examining barristers learn how to ask questions and to have a certain kind of intuition which will turn half-formed conjectures into a satisfying, amply illustrated, account of the links which go back from an outcome.

* * *

Much of Descartes' method is still useful for the social scientist; dividing up the problem, starting from the known and so on. It is just that it tends to get over-emphasized in our education as the way to solve problems whereas, in reality, it is just one way and best suited to the physical, laboratory, sciences.

The distinction between forward and backward reasoning is indeed very important. With forward reasoning plus experiments it is much easier to provide proofs. We guess and if the guess works we seem to be right and get closer to the truth until we finally are right – as in games such as Hangman, Submarines, 'Black Box' and other children's games which are based on guessing patterns, firing questions or testing the guesses, and ending up with the truth.

Yet this method clearly does not work in discovering the cause of many of the things that interests us, the big problems. Why do people fall in love, why do they kill each other, why is there so much inequality in the world, why did the scientific revolution occur first in Europe and not China? All these sorts of question, the ones in *Letters to Lily*, cannot be solved by the Cartesian method. Nor are the answers very high on a scale of reliable knowledge. The best we can hope for is a persuasive, quite convincing, or at the least plausible answer – perhaps above the threshold of 'beyond reasonable doubt.'

And Holmes is probably right that while most of us are pretty good at conjecturing forwards (we have to be in order to survive) the skill of reasoning backwards is far less stressed or taught and hence needs more attention. We can get by, on the whole, with fairly rough ideas of why things have happened in the past, or currently exist – though it raises our curiosity. Yet only a few professionals have the skills, energy and time to probe deep here. So it is worth picking up some elementary skills which will be useful in giving preliminary solutions to all sorts of things.

* * *

The world is very complex; sensations are endless. How do we separate out what is essential from what is not when we are searching for the solution to a problem? To a certain extent successful hunting depends on simplifying, on winnowing away the irrelevant. This is one of the principal aims of a laboratory, and it is why glass is so essential for laboratories, for it keeps out the contagion and confusion of the world. All 'matter out of place' is banished by white coats, scrubbed surfaces, clear glass. These are the hallmarks of the traditional 'laboratory.'

Although a social scientist's 'laboratory' or study often looks chaotic, and sometimes dirty – it performs the same function. Some matter (books, ideas) are allowed in, while a great deal is excluded. The principles of inclusion and exclusion are worth looking into more carefully.

There are various ways to narrow down the range of causes. One is the device of starting with a list of all possible causes and then going through them deleting all those that are impossible until whatever remains must be the cause however implausible. This is both a good and a delusory method. It is good because it forces us to bring things out into the open, to formalize, to run all reasonable hypotheses through the mind. It may also be good for the main reason that it is advocated, namely that it gives confidence that an unlikely hypothesis may be correct.

Let me give an example from the book I wrote with Gerry Martin on *The Glass Bathyscaphe: How Glass Changed the World*. There has been much speculation about why there occurred the two great interlinked revolutions, the Renaissance and the Scientific Revolution, both increasing reliable knowledge about the world. Why did they happen where they did (western Europe), when they did (c.1350–1650), and at all (and in the shape they did)?

Now if we use the Holmsian method of exclusion, we can go through all the causes advanced – wealth, revival of learning, cities, printing press, foreign exploration and others, and show that none of them in themselves work. We can eliminate them all, as some have done. What can we then do? Is there something that only happened there, then, and whose form fits with the revolution? We guessed it was the glass revolution.

Now glass is, on the face of it, a long shot – a fact shown by the fact that no-one previously (with the partial exception of Lewis Mumford) has ever suggested this. But our confidence in the plausibility is increased by the elimination of all other possible causes. We can ask – do you have a better idea? So Holmes' method of exclusion has some definite benefits.

Unfortunately, however the method is weakened by one simple danger or error. For it assumes that the list of possible causes upon which it is based will include the correct solution, however implausible. While Holmes stresses that all possible ideas must be included, it is not usually feasible to do that. Any thinker will probably generate only a few of the potential explanations. The more unlikely, the less likely he or she will be to include such an explanation. Let me illustrate from another book.

The doctor Thomas McKeown explicitly set out to use the Holmsian method of exclusion in his book *The Modern Rise of Population*. The problem was this. Why did the death rate suddenly start to drop in England in the middle of the eighteenth century when we would have expected it to rise (because of cities, the miseries of industrial labour and other factors).

McKeown listed the possible causes. These were a sudden change in the pathogens (microbes); a change in the environment (housing, clothing, drainage); a change in medical knowledge and techniques (medicine, hospitals); a change in the food supply. It was not difficult for McKeown to demolish the first three as impossible causes, for none of them occurred on a sufficient scale, if at all, to explain the drop in death rates. What was left was nutrition. However implausible, this must be the cause.

His book was published in 1978. Within ten years, detailed studies of the height and weight of the British population after 1750, alongside studies of nutritional intake, showed that, if anything, the nutritional standards of the British population had declined during the eighteenth century. His only remaining solution was not only implausible, but disproved. There was no explanation left.

It was like a final revelation, when the detective goes through the list of suspects and shows that it could not have been the maid, the landlord, the cook, and then turns triumphantly to accuse the butler. Then the butler quietly announces that he had forgotten to mention that he had spent the day of the murder at a butler's conference, and many could witness to that. There is no suspect left.

I was faced with this problem and, to may own satisfaction, solved McKeown's problem by the simple expedient of going back along a chain of causation. What was the main disease that declined – dysentery. What mainly causes dysentery – polluted water. What happened to drinking habits around the 1750s – a new drink, tea, was rapidly taking off. Was there anything special about tea – the water is boiled, and tea contains a strong anti-septic (phenolics), which kills the bacteria which cause dysentery.

So, if we add tea to the list, however implausible it may seem at first sight to argue that tea allowed the modern rise of population in England, without which there could not have been an industrial revolution, we find that the humble camellia leaf is what made our modern world possible. This explanation will stand until such time as someone shows that it could not have been tea, or suggests something better.

The point is obvious. The method of exclusion acts as a sort of razor. It cuts away the unnecessary. It is the artist's brush, the writer's correcting pen, the sculptor's knife. It trims and excludes leaving only the necessary and the true. Yet it only works if the first list contains the solution, or at least a convincing and possible solution.

FIVE

Evidence

'Problems cannot be solved at the same level of thinking that created them'

'He who can no longer pause to wonder and stand rapt in awe

is as good as dead; his eyes are closed'

'The whole of science is nothing more than the refinement of everyday thinking'

'Education is the progressive realization of our ignorance'

—ALBERT EINSTEIN

D EAR ROSA,

The secret of successful research is to get the right balance between conjecture and data. Too much conjecture, or too powerful conjectures, can lead us to manufacture and manipulate data. It must be possible for data to modify or destroy conjectures.

On the other hand, too much data can have a damaging effect. Like too much ballast in a balloon, it may prevent lift off, or at least keep the balloon hovering at a low level where very little can be seen. To continue the balloon analogy, sometimes we need to release ballast (data), so that the mind can see vast distances and the shape of countries and continents. Then we need to add data so that we skim low and see the birds in the trees.

This rising and falling in our enquiry requires constant vigilance since there is a strong temptation to move to one extreme or the other. It is delightful to float at a great height and speculate on the fate of the world, or global history as it is now called. This means we can forgo the toilsome effort of searching for, storing and struggling with, detailed facts. It is equally attractive to put down our head, become fascinated by some sub-problem, so that we do not have to worry about the perturbing wider picture. Most people, indeed, travel along at the middle level, neither high nor low. This is the safest course, least dangerous but also least likely to lead to any interesting new discoveries. The great explorers take risks and swing high and low.

* * *

The need to swoop very low is stressed again and again by Sherlock Holmes and other detectives. Whether we use artificial devices (often made of glass) which both allow and force the eye to see the detail, such as microscopes, magnifying glasses, cameras, which arrest time, zoom lenses in filming we must force ourselves to get up really close. The discovery, like the Devil, is very often in the detail.

If a problem is very difficult to solve, it is often because reality looks normal on the surface or at a middle distance. The tell-tale deviation is often tiny, invisible to most people. Thus the great progress of the second half of the nineteenth century, whether in medicine (Koch, Pasteur) or biology (Darwin, Wallace) came through the development of the microscopic eye which saw beneath the bland surface of things. Holmes and others are full of this method.

By coming up very close to things, the ordinary often becomes extraordinary, excites wonder, surprise and admiration, the three emotions which Adam Smith thought lay behind all good research. Another strong theme in the detective method is the need to make the normal seem abnormal, to question everything. In a way this links to the theme of much science writing, of the need for a child-like vision. A walk with a child is often a delight because he or she notices so much. When you were a child, Rosa, and I took you on walks, we would stop every few yards while you picked up and examined a flower, stone, insect, leaf, or sometimes even more exciting things like an old pair of blue sunglasses left in an allotment. You wanted to examine it, keep it, take it home, know more about why it is as it is. As we grow up the sensations and experiences multiply and we consign all this to the normal, the expected, and hence the invisible.

All of us know this from travel. The first visit to almost anywhere is rich and amazing, everything is fresh and new. The mystery and strangeness quickly wears off after the second or third visit.

What detectives and researchers have to do is encourage that sense of wonder and strangeness, of puzzlement at the apparently normal. Holmes is full of admonitions to Watson to this effect. Indeed he takes it to the extreme of arguing that the hardest case to solve is when almost everything is entirely normal and ordinary. Only minute observation will sometimes reveal a tiny clue of something abnormal, all the more striking because it is so tiny and sticks out from the expected. These are very significant clues.

Related to this is some advice about some of the tricks or disguises which conceals these clues so that they evade almost everyone. One is that the facts are too obvious, too much in the line of sight, so that we do not see them. Edgar Allen Poe's story *The Purloined Letter*, where the sought-for letter is in the most obvious place (the letter rack on the desk in the centre of the room) is the best known case. This is like many scientific discoveries which, after the fact, appear trivial because they are right under our noses.

My experience of studying both glass and tea are cases in point. Both are so close that we do not see them. In the former case, when I had the idea that glass was the major factor behind the Renaissance and the Scientific Revolution, I used to pose a puzzle to intelligent groups dining at King's College, including historians of art.

I would point to a table laden with glasses and say that the clue as to why and when these great events occurred in western Europe was on the table. A long period would elapse while people would suggest forks, silver, table cloths and other things before they finally *noticed* the most ubiquitous and commonplace object on the table – glass.

It is all another example of Confucius' remark that it would not be a fish that discovered water, or a bird that discovered air. The more obvious, and more important, a thing is, the more we are likely to take it for granted and not to notice it. Hence the advice to start with the most obvious explanation is a good one.

Yet how do we see the over-obvious? There are two techniques worth mentioning. One is used by Dupin and Holmes. They spend a lot of effort setting up a detailed picture of the normal, flat, expected, set of features in the world. They make mental back-drops which are very explicit, measuring rods, if we change the metaphor. Against this, something slightly odd immediately stands out. If the backdrop is white and grey, a tiny green or red object will become visible. If there is no back-drop, nothing stands out.

Two variants of this have been developed in the social sciences. One is the setting up of 'ideal types' or simplified models, as in the sociologist Max Weber's work. These set out the possibilities – the simplified forms of authority, rationality and so on. Then he used these as thinking models which when applied to particular cases showed interesting deviations and noticeable exceptions.

The main defect of these ideal types is that they are static, which means they are not very well suited to either historical investigation or the understanding of future events. In *Letters to Lily* I developed the theory of tendencies, taken from Lord Acton, J. S. Mill and others, which I think also lies behind much forensic science.

This is the idea that although there are not immutable laws, either of human nature or of history, there are likelihoods. We can say that we can have conjectures about the way in which, all else being equal, things will happen. J. S. Mill gives examples; a big man will tend to be brave, a person with a vested interest will tend to be biased. But these are only statistical probabilities, to which there are many exceptions.

If we identify tendencies, we can then see the deviations. So power tends to corrupt, human populations tend to grow, resources tend to be used up, humans tend to fight, knowledge tends to expand. These are our moving ideal types or gauges. We take them to an intriguing case and we find that sometimes they do not work. There is some unexplained deviation. This suggests a mystery. So, for example, mortality tends to rise with congested cities, yet suddenly in eighteenth century England this tendency did not work itself out. Why? We are alerted to things that move against the grain.

It is this 'against the grain' of things which is at the heart of much of the most important scientific and other discoveries. Most people do not notice, but the explicitly trained eye begins to do so.

* * *

A second and important method is comparison and travel. As we become acclimatized to our world, the water of everyday experience in which we learn to swim becomes invisible and hence unexaminable. One way suddenly to become aware of it again is to travel. Like the first fish climbing up onto the beaches, we become aware that there are other elements, that water is not a given fact. We develop lungs to process air and, in the shock of the encounter, for a while we are suspended between worlds and are aware of both water and air.

This seems to me to be one of the principal values of travel and of its formalized and instituted version, social anthropology. It destabilizes our world and turns what we have learnt to take as natural, normal and unquestionable, into something that is cultural, abnormal and highly questionable.

This was a quality of travel, or at least wide reading, beautifully described by Montaigne in the sixteenth century and Pascal a century later; namely that most of the things which we hold as normal, invariable, the only way to do or perceive things, are in fact idiosyncratic, variable, mutable. So truth, beauty, personality, gender, power, almost everything becomes questionable.

It may be that because of a combination of globalization (and mass media) and the rapidity of change in most societies, this is a lesson we do not need as much. Indeed, we need more encouragement to have confidence that the way we do things today, odd though it is, is a perfectly reasonable and viable way. It is a matter of balance.

Certainly in the consideration of many topics, comparison soon makes us aware of intriguing puzzles and normalities of which we would not otherwise be aware of. I had no idea of how very individualistic the English were until I spent time in Nepal. I did not know how important glass was in the west until I realized that it had faded out in most of the rest of the world after the middle ages. I had no realization of how war-like and nationalistic European states were until I looked at Chinese and Japanese history over the last thousand years.

* * *

What this method of comparison is particularly important for is to alert us to the very most difficult things to discover and realize the significance of, that is silences, absences, things that do not happen. We do not normally notice non-events, non-noise, non-sights. They are unnoticeable, inaudible, invisible. Our senses do not easily register them, though, as animals, we are aware when things are 'unnaturally quiet' or 'unnaturally static.'

Holmes and others developed a stress on the proverbial 'dog that did not bark in the night' or, in slightly less well-known incidents, the dead passenger on the train who was not carrying a ticket, or the single dumb-bell.

The absences here are tiny and very difficult to notice. They are equally difficult to notice if they are huge. The absence of a belief in a single God, a God who created the world according to strict laws and principles which underly most of existence (in China or Japan) has hampered the growth of scientific knowledge in the western sense. Yet if we just looked at those civilizations we might not have noticed the absence. The absence of glass instruments had huge effects in China and Japan.

In reverse, the absence of bamboo, mulberry paper and rice made certain developments impossible in western civilizations. The absence of the sign and concept of the zero in western Europe until the twelfth century is another, as is the absence of the printing press in Islamic civilizations, after it was banned. The absence of traditional social classes in America or of castes in England – the list is almost endless.

Very often it is these silences, absences, missing things which are the key to understanding. We are intrigued to know why they are not there – why did the people who early on imported the tea (the Dutch, French) not drink it much? – and we are intrigued by the possible consequences of the absence.

The interpretation of absences and silences needs several qualifications. Not every absence is equally significant. Absences cannot easily be put forward as the major reason why something else did not happen. We know that it would be ridiculous to say that the reason I have not travelled to Manchester in the last month is because there is no direct flight from Cambridge to Manchester, no direct railway line, no clear motorway. I could get there, but there is no particular reason for doing so – in other words an absence may provide a barrier, or even an insuperable one. Yet it may not be the principal reason for something else.

Thus we could plausibly argue that without scientific instruments the Chinese and Japanese could not have had a scientific revolution. Yet when these became available from the middle of the seventeenth century there was still no scientific revolution. Many other things are involved. The Greeks knew about steam engines – as toys. They did not develop them as labour-saving devices.

Nevertheless, the discussion of absences and of tiny deviations from the expected does illuminate the need for conjectures. It is the conjectures, the models based on experience and reading, the ideal types, the science of locating tendencies which brings things into relief.

All of this, as Einstein and others have pointed out, is only a refinement, a formalization, of ordinary thinking. Any infant or child is deploying these techniques and adults use them all the time. A mother notices when the expected cry of an infant is not there. A child notices when the expected background burble of the television stops. We notice when the heating goes off, or the silence of the birds before a storm. It is just that while we build up a set of implicit and partial models of how things should be, the tendencies and patterns, and these guide our lives, scientists develop a set of particular formalized methods in their specific field.

It is like sport. Engaging in a physical sport we develop muscles 'we didn't know we had.' The muscles were there all the time, but with use they become stronger. Researchers develop mental muscles, as did that lean and fit prodigy Sherlock Holmes. They develop their 'nose', the sharpness of their eyes, the speed of their thought. Yet it is just a matter of being aware of what is necessary, the goals, and then application and training.

* * *

Holmes and others developed a wide range of techniques. One was a form of broad, sometimes called 'lateral', thinking. Holmes stressed that bits of information which others discarded as quite irrelevant to the current situation might turn out to be very important through a long chain of connection. This is indeed true.

It is a feature of all deep research that it is a matter of connecting the hitherto unconnected. It has not been connected because the two things are separated. This is often because of the current framework of thought, or because of physical separation. Most people do not and cannot see the connection. Many of the most fruitful minds are those like Francis Bacon, Einstein, J.M. Keynes, who are have wide interests and read in diverse fields.

These people are specialists, but also generalists. They allow themselves to go up very high in the balloon and to look across whole continents. When they do this they notice something beyond the mountains, perhaps the start of a river whose source has never been understood, perhaps a tribe very similar and obviously once connected to another on our side of the mountains. The low level balloonist would never see any of this. They bring these long-range, widely separated factors into connection and make a major breakthrough.

There is a cost to all of this activity. Our energy and time is finite and we cannot know everything. As we stray elsewhere we can lose touch with our speciality or become out of date. It is a risky activity. Furthermore, the more diverse the information, the more difficult it is to retrieve any specific piece.

So filing systems and organisation of knowledge become an obsession – as we see with the anthropologist Sir James Frazer or Charles Darwin.

Success also requires a lot of intuition to be able to go straight to the heart of relevant, but widely separated, fields and to store away what might be useful in the future. This also is a risky, long-term, venture. Often the prizes and the head-start goes to the sprinter. They concentrate on a delimited field, master it, and rush off with the rewards. The rewards may be middling, but their career and reputation and life is made. They have quickly climbed a middling sized mountain which bears their name.

Often to achieve the really magnificent feats, the Himalayas of the mind, takes many years of unrewarded, patient, ill-paid, toil. There are examples which will be worth looking at. The silent labours of Montesquieu, Adam Smith, Tocqueville, Darwin, are emblems of this. Special self-confidence, security, dedication are needed and it is not a path for all.

There are cases of people who switched into a new field in the middle of their life and became enormously learned – Sir Joseph Needham the biologist and expert on China is an example. Yet it is usually the case that it was around your age that Einstein, Newton, Tocqueville or others had a vision which they solidly followed until they stood astride the mountain whose peak was above the clouds and gazed round on immortality.

We have to plan (as many of us are now fortunate enough to be able to do) for a marathon, rather than a sprint. That is to say, we need to think about how to set up a life style, an expanding and flexible environment, which will enable us to keep climbing.

In climbing a very high mountain, it is no good to rush at it.

To do so would lead to exhaustion on the lower slopes. There are stores to be accumulated, techniques to be practiced, equipment to be assembled. Slowly and deliberately, with a team of others, we move from camp to camp, using everyday skills to do the non-everyday.

The same is true if we use the metaphor of the sailing journey. Captain Cook achieved what he did through forethought, good planning, good navigation, intuition and skills with people. He was just an ordinary working-class lad without any special education. Yet he discovered new worlds through self-belief and slow, careful, thought. This all started when he was your age, Rosa.

There is nothing to stop any of us, as long as we separate off the long and the short term. We have to live and it is no good becoming so obsessive about the long term that we give up the daily bread and butter. We will starve on the lower slopes. So we can look at the long-term as a hobby, a bi-pursuit, the building up of the resources.

* * *

The mind is not only a comparitor – that is it works best by being flooded with comparisons and contrasts – but it is also, like the body, most effective when it alternates between action and rest. Almost all the great break-throughs have occurred in moments of rest – at dawn, on a walk, on a journey, while listening to music. It is not difficult to realize why this should be the case.

What we do is to focus, concentrate, work out what the question is and load our mind with relevant, possible, data or resources from the area where we think the answer might lie.

But it is no good then thinking logically and hard. A chain of logic will not lead to the answer. By definition, if this were possible, others who have strained to do so at their desks (and there are many) would have found the solution. What Weber pointed out is that we do not find the answer at our formal work-place.

We know this from the anecdotes of Darwin, Wallace, Poincaré and Einstein, and many others. The distant connection, the Eureka moment, occurred in rest or at least when on a journey or doing something entirely different. The stretched mind had slackened and as it did so, suddenly something 'clicked' is the frequent metaphor. This is encapsulated in the motto 'solvitur ambulando', 'it is solved in walking.'

Just the physical diversion of walking, of alcohol, of a bath or shower, of going into or out of sleep, seems to put our mind in that relaxed state where, like Yeats' poem the 'Long-legged fly', the 'mind moves upon silence.'

There must be as little friction, obstacles, impediments as possible. And commonly these obstacles and impediments include those things we might think would be most useful, that is 'data' and 'facts', the logical procedures and analytic and rigorous rationality of the mind.

We can have too many clogging facts which, like trees, prevent us from seeing the wood. We can be too rational and strain too hard to 'solve' problems so that we do not see the easy and obvious solutions which burst in on us in a moment of repose. 'Thinking paths' as in Darwin's garden, or the Kyoto Philosopher's Walk, literal and metaphorical walks, are essential for us and we should cultivate diversions. Only a certain amount of time should be allotted to 'work', or rather we have to learn that 'work' does not stop at our desk, and learn to lead lives in which work and life are blended.

SIX

Creative Writing

'It should be possible to explain the laws of physics to a barmaid'
'Not everything that counts can be counted,
and not everything that can be counted counts'
'Learn from yesterday, live for today, hope for tomorrow.
The important thing is not to stop questioning'
'I think and think for months and years. Nintey-nine times
the conclusion is false. The hundredth time I am right'

—ALBERT EINSTEIN

D EAR ROSA,

My major mentors, scientists like Einstein and Poincaré, detectives like Holmes and Dupin, give a great deal of help in trying to understand how we can discover things through, experiments, cross-questioning and forming of mental models. They speak less of the process of arranging materials and communicating what we have found to others. This re-enforces the image which many have that 'writing up' is largely a matter of summarizing what we already know.

'Writing up' is an active piece of exploration, a second fieldwork, except in the mind rather than in the 'field.' In what some people call the 'remembered village' of our mind, we do our best work, abstracted from clogging detail. It is here that we either do or do not make sense of things and find out what it is we are really trying to find out. It is the really creative moment, the magical alchemy, like the potter's kiln or the chemist's retort. It does not just firm up and organize, but transforms and transmutes base things and makes them into something new and different.

This is so obvious in relation to painting, poetry, music and mathematics, that it is surprising that the false analogies with 'digging things up' from history and archaeology have made us forget it. Of course there is often a good deal of description, narration, classification and sorting out. But if work stops at this level the result will be mechanical and not very inspiring.

What is needed is to encourage the art of creating, connecting, exploring 'at the tip of the pen' (as Yeats put it), or in the fingers on the keyboard. It is that moment in Handel's garret in Dublin as he composed the Messiah in a few weeks, or Leonardo as he painted, or Poincaré as he solved an impossibly difficult mathematical problem.

Since it is so complex and so magical, all I can do is to suggest both from my own and other's experiences, a few of the things which encourage this creativity. If you are very fortunate, you will experience these moments, which you have often known as a child in your games, but which now can last for weeks and months. They are when we seem to gaze into eternity and the world suddenly becomes clear and calm.

* * *

There are a few very obvious but basic things about sustained creative work habits which I learnt early on and though I sometimes break the rules, generally guide me.

One is to do with space. It is important to have a place or places which are associated with writing, in bed for the diary, the desk for typing up, an easy chair for original writing. If we look at some great thinkers they all worked in ways that would help their creativity; Maitland at a lectern as if he were lecturing, Adam Smith dictating as he walked up and down or in a comfortable chair with a very small table beside him, Tocqueville in an easy chair. It is very important that the body should be comfortable and all the clutter of the unnecessary taken away.

This is why I am writing this in the Summer House, in the streaming sun, even though it is mid-December, or why I wrote the first few *Letters to Lily* in our bedroom. The barn, full of books and data and computers is a good place for the second writing, the typing and the revisions, but there are constant distractions – there are too many trees to be able to see the wood.

Then there is the question of how we write. This is very personal. My earlier writing was mainly on a typewriter. The second draft had to be completely re-typed as did every subsequent draft. So I improved a great deal from draft to draft. This filtering has disappeared with word processors which produce a more or less perfect-looking (and spell-checked) version straight away. This makes it difficult to improve very much from version to version; tinkering seems both unnecessary and a big effort.

Although it slows things down – perhaps its great advantage – I now only go straight to the 'typing into a computer' when I am writing short pieces, reviews or articles. Serious writing, like this set of letters, I write by hand with a pen. This forces me to re-type it and at that stage it can be expanded or shrunk, the expression improved, new ideas inserted. It is a partial re-writing. It also means that it is easier to insert bits of writing done on a journey or elsewhere, when thoughts come but the laptop computer is not at hand.

There are other advantages. Even with the best of computers there is a danger of losing files. A hand-written version is the securest back-up. Also, perhaps because of my background, although I am a touch typist and can work fast without noticing the computer very much, it is always there. Simultaneously one is writing and being presented with what one has written. One mis-types more often than one mis-writes, so there are constant interruptions to go back and get it looking good, correct typos and grammar etc. This is taking away some of the energy that should be going into creativity. And there is usually a hardly audible electronic buzz which is distracting.

One of my needs in writing is peace, though I know of other people (like my historian uncle) who can only work with background noise. Yeats' poem, 'Long Legged Fly', describes beautifully the peace and seclusion which Caesar, Helen of Troy and Michelangelo needed so that their minds 'could move upon silence.' As the poet Coleridge illustrated when he lost most of 'Kubla Khan' through the unfortunate intrusion of the man from Porlock, the mind is like delicate gossamer webs of complex associations when it is creating. Unwanted noise, or intrusive anxieties can very easily ruin this.

This may be one of the reasons why many of the great ideas occur in baths, bed, in a bus or coach, all places of seclusion. When writing we should try to set up a visible, or invisible, wall around ourselves where there is as little disturbance as possible.

One difficulty is that even if the children, the friends, the television are banished for a while, the mind disturbs itself. Two of these disturbances are particularly undermining. One is sudden unrelated thoughts and often worries – 'oh, I should write to so and so', 'oh, I must buy some more toothpaste and so on.'

I have found from experience that before starting to write it is helpful to have another sheet of paper, or, even better, some small slips, beside me. On these I jot down these intrusive thoughts. I think I learnt this at an evangelical Christian boy's camp as a technique to deal with what I was told would be the 'Devil's' interruptions when I was trying to pray. Once written down, the thought can be put on one side and dealt with later.

A second obstacle is the feeling that we cannot proceed unless we do something else first. Often this is clearly just an excuse, which comes from the fact that writing and thinking is hard work and, as Yeats put it, 'All things can tempt me from the craft of verse.' We want to be tempted, and if the temptation is an apparently reasonable one, such as the feeling that we cannot possibly write another word until we have read something in the library, or checked on the internet, or talked to someone, it is very difficult to resist. Even the desire to go off and consult our own notes can lead to several hours interruption and the thread can be lost.

So I advise myself and my students to separate off the process of creative writing from the task of searching for data. If in my writing I come to a place where evidence or further consultation is needed, I make a guess and a note to myself to check something later. It is important to keep on with the sketch, even if certain things are missing, so 'to check' or 'to read X and Y' are put in and I work around the obstacle, to come back later to it. C.S. Lewis said research is like eating a fish; the bony parts could be taken out and put on the edge of the plate, to be dealt with carefully after the main part had been eaten.

* * *

Another thing I have found helpful is to work on several different pieces of creative work at once. The mind is multi-tasking
and works better, I have found, on parallel problems. So usually
I am working on a number of intellectual tasks simultaneously,
for example, several different chapters of a book, several different books, and several different stages in the writing and
re-typing of a work I am engaged on.

This has several advantages. If I am working on not just one
but several chapters of a book or thesis, if I become stuck on
one, I can leave it and move to another which may be more
promising. We always get stuck and it often only requires leaving
something for a while to solve the problem. The mind finds a
way round without being forced. If we are only going down
one path, we will be blocked. If we go down several simultaneously, we will progress all the time. We often find that we come
back from behind the problem, and it has been outflanked and
solved by working on something else. Each of us is an army
of skills and potentials and not just a single soldier, we should
advance on a broad front and not in single files when we can
easily be ambushed or trapped.

Another advantage of working on several things at once is
that different tasks require different types of concentration. To
be writing the first draft of something, the first cutting through
the undergrowth, is the most tiring and difficult. All is fresh and
overgrown and confused. Anthony Trollope rightly warned that
we should not ever write at this high intensity for more than
three hours a day. If we were to write for just these three hours,
even a slow writer will produce about two thousand words a

day, and hence in five days ten thousand words. In theory, it should be possible to write an eighty-thousand word book or thesis in two months, leaving the week-ends free! I have occasionally done something like this, but it seldom seems to works quite like this.

In fact, as well as working on the first draft of several different bits, there are other tasks. There is the typing in of the second version, or the reading through of a draft to make amendments, or the further reading and research. All these tasks need to be shuffled and varied over the day and weeks.

I have learned that it is best to work in parallel, rather than in blocks. It looks logical to write for a month, then spend a month reading or indexing, and then back to writing. Yet this does not work so well for me. I find I can only write at full concentration for about two or three hours on a first draft. Since my best time for writing is about 8–11AM, the creaming off of the best intellectual energy each day is far better than spending a week trying to write for six hours a day so that the next week I can read for six hours a day. So I ration my writing, but try to make sure that I stick at it.

Once we have allocated our best mental time to writing (for others it is late at night or early in the morning) that still leaves another four or five hours when the mind is active. If I am not teaching, administering, or, increasingly, answering emails, then I try to do a diversity of things, some reading (again I find two or three hours a day is enough), some note taking or indexing, some teaching or talking to people.

Many people produce their best work alongside a busy life of administration, teaching, and other activities. This is perhaps partly because they are forced into this multi-tasking mode. It is tempting to believe that if only we could retire and 'write all the time', instead of suffering the constant interruptions, we would produce much more and better work and open up a new chapter of creativity. From my experience and observation this is not true.

Those who have not created when engaged in many things, do not usually do so once they leave the strenuous life. Those who create while 'in harness', as they say, usually continue to do so, though it is often noticeable that often their best work is done before they 'retire.' If one wants to get something done, ask a busy man; the more a person has to do, the more they seem to get done.

* * *

Another reason for the heightened creativity under pressure is related to the need to 'write first, think later.' Great artists, painters, poets, musicians, create almost subconsciously or by instinct. We can easily become over-cerebral, over rational, over conscious as we learn the craft. This is a necessary stage, but gradually it should become more instinctive. We hesitate, we try to get everything straight in our minds, everything sorted out first, and then to write. This often turns into a form of 'writer's block.'

I had this disease quite badly for a number of years. Being of only average ability, I knew that my undergraduate essays and later the drafts of my doctorate could only have a chance of competing with those of my brighter colleagues if I tried really hard and used superior organisation. So I would not start to write until I had assembled a very detailed plan, down to the paragraph level. Each paragraph was mapped out and suitable quotes and arguments written out. Then the whole was embarked on. There was little spontaneity in most of the writing, though it did help to give a plausible semblance of intelligence.

It is obvious that some ideas, plans, plots are necessary before writing. But certainly as we gain confidence and experience, there is a wonderful liberation, and hopefully improvement, in our writing. We put down more of what we ourselves think, and then modify and delete it in the light of further thought and evidence.

As Kipling put it, the idea is to release one's 'daemon' or demon, the amazing inner compulsion which seems to write through us. The mind needs to be set fee. Curiously this is best done by not putting too much emphasis on formal thinking. It is like many high level activities, like 'Zen and the Art of Archery', or playing the piano at concert level. We have to learn the skills to such a point that we no longer have to think about them. Imagine what a pianist would sound like if she had to consciously think before choosing to play each note. The same with writing. The great poets describe how whole stanzas of poems come into their minds fully formed, and scientists describe the same phenomenon.

In order to do this we have to have both confidence and enthusiasm in what we are doing. If we over-work or write, or have other deep worries, that undermines energy and enthusiasm and the writing suffers, and this then feeds back into the anxiety. Obviously I cannot write about those wider things, love life, friendship, money worries, job worries, health worries, which sap or encourage us, though I have touched on some of them in *Letters to Lily.*

* * *

I'd like to end by quoting part of a letter which the great writer on Japan, Lafcadio Hearn, wrote about the way in which he wrote. His books are models of clarity and insight and he worked out a way to take most of the strain out of writing by dividing the very difficult process into several parts. I think if you follow this advice, you will find writing much easier and more enjoyable.

'*I go to work in this way. The subject is before me; I can't bother even thinking about it. That would tire me too much. I simply arrange the notes and write down whatever part of the subject most pleases me first. I write hurriedly without care.*

Then I put the MS [manuscript] aside for the day, and do something else more agreeable.

Next day I read over the pages written, correct, and write them all over again. In the course of doing this, quite mechanically new thoughts come up, errors make themselves felt, improvements are suggested. I stop.

Next day, I re-write the third time. This is the test time. The result is a great improvement usually – but not perfection.

I then take clean paper, and begin to make the final copy. Usually this has to be done twice.

In the course of four to five rewritings, the whole though reshapes itself, and the whole style is changed and fixed. The work has done itself, developed, grown; it would have been very different had I trusted to the first thought. But I let the thought define and crystallize itself. Perhaps you will say this is too much trouble. I used to think so. But the result is amazing. The average is five perfect pages a day, with about two or three hours work. By the other method one or two pages a day are extremely difficult to write. Indeed I do not think I could write one perfect page a day, by thinking out everything as I write. The mental strain is too much.

The fancy is like a horse that goes well without whip or spur, and refuses duty if either are used.

By petting it and leaving it free, it surpasses desire.

I know when the page is fixed by a sort of focusing it takes – when the first impression has returned, after all corrections, more forcibly than at first felt, and in half the space first occupied.

To those with whom writing is almost an automatic exertion, the absolute fatigue is no more than that of writing a letter. The rest of the work DOES ITSELF, *without your effort. It is like spiritualism. Just move the pen, and the ghosts do the wording.*

Another important thing is to take the most agreeable part of the subject first. Order is of no earthly consequence, but a great hindrance. The success of this part gives encouragement, and curiously develops the idea of the relative parts.'[1]

I have to do much excision of 'verys,' 'that's' and 'whiches' – to murder adjectives and adverbs – to modify verbs.

Print, of course, is the great test. Colour only comes out in proof – never in MS. I can't get anything perfect in MS. A friend is invaluable.

---

1 *The Japanese Letters of Lafcadio Hearn*, ed. With intro by ELIZABETH BISLAND (Constable, London, 1911), pp. 42–44, 58–9.

SEVEN

Conditions for Creativity

'The legs are the wheels of creativity'
'The secret to creatitivity is knowing how to hide your sources'
'I know quite certainly that I myself have no special talent;
curiosity, obsession and dogged endurance, combined
with self-criticism have brought me to my ideas'
'We should take care not to make the intellect our god;
it has, of course, powerful muscles, but no personality'

—ALBERT EINSTEIN

D EAR ROSA,

Although it seems logical to write in the order of the projected work, starting with a preface, chapter one, chapter two and proceeding on, in fact it is better to start somewhere in the middle, where the hub or centre of interest will be.

If I am lighting a fire, I do not start with the bigger, thicker, possibly wetter and more difficult branches, but with whatever will catch light most easily. Once this is alight, I can add thicker bits to the flame.

So start with whatever really excites you, the bit you think is the most entrancing, intriguing, amazing and mysterious. Then work out from that as the mind dictates. Do not start from the boring edges of a painting, but from the striking centre and then work out. This will help prevent artist's block and as you write or create you will gain confidence and excitement, which should grow until, without really noticing it, most of the work is roughed out. You can then tackle the most difficult and important pieces, the introduction and the conclusion, both of which should be written at the end.

Once the mind is aflame, let the flames leap as they wish. Do not try to limit or direct them too much. In other words, in Kipling's words, 'never write short.' Even if the writing goes in unpredictable directions and seems to be taking you away from your main aim, let it flow. It can always be pruned, cut, used elsewhere. But creative, excited, 'following the scent' writings, is a precious thing. When the mind is in full chase it should be encouraged, not reined in. Writing as a 'second fieldwork' or discovery pursues clues and ideas as you write, in an amazing but subterranean way. Have trust in it and it may well come up in a strange, new, beautiful and fresh valley.

In other words, do not worry in the first draft about word lengths, chapter lengths, days elapsing before you get onto what you think is the real subject. The periods of writing enthusiasm never last for ever and often suddenly stop. When they do so, like a light switch being turned off as Kipling puts it, there is no point in forcing the mind on. Stop there and start or continue with something else. 'The wind bloweth where it listeth', as the Bible says, and inspiration, literally the blowing into the mind, cannot be forced. All we can do is prepare for it and provide propitious conditions for the butterfly to alight a while. As it flutters around your mind, treasure it.

* * *

If I am using a bonfire to burn a lot of rubbish over several days, I do not let the fire go out completely overnight. At the end of a day I leave a few half-burnt logs smouldering. It is much easier to start a new fire by raking over these live ashes and adding more wood rather than from scratch.

The same is true of creative work. I learnt long ago from W.G. Hoskins the local historian that if I was going to leave some writing, for a night, and more especially for a few days, I should resist the temptation to tidily finish off a chapter or section. Starting at a blank page titled 'Chapter 3' at nine o'clock on a Monday morning after a break freezes the mind and makes it very difficult to get going.

It is much better to do most of the work, but leave a little bit to be done, with some brief notes as to where you think you will next go. Then, with the still half-hot argument raked over by re-reading the last few paragraphs you wrote, plus the indications of what to write next in your notes, you can continue for a few hours. The mind is now heated up and the transition to a new chapter or section feels much easier.

* * *

When you are in fully creative mood, ideas may come thick and fast. Hopefully they will form at 'the tip of your pen', but you will find that they also come at unexpected times through the day and night. Again they are often very transitory. Though you think you will remember them, they often flit off unless recorded. Especially in that precious moment between sleeping and waking in the morning when many ideas seem suddenly to crowd into the mind.

When I am in a creative mood, I try to carry a pen and small notebook, or even just some scraps of paper, with me. The philosopher Thomas Hobbes always went for a walk with a walking stick which opened up at the top to reveal an ink-well and quill. With that and some paper he could capture the thoughts which, in John Aubrey's words, 'darted into his mind.'

My mother tells me that from my early teens I used to carry a small tin filled with cards in it around with me. I called it pretentiously my 'Great Thoughts' box, which was later replaced by other similar systems. I now have little piles of paper around me to write on, as well as notebooks of various sizes.

I have noted that productive people of the generation above me, a number of eminent scientists, seize envelopes, committee agendas or whatever is at hand and start to scribble on them. Thoughts are obviously darting into their minds. This is one of the joys of creativity. It is like fishing. You set the bait, relax, sit back, and, when you least expect it, there is a strong tug and you reel in to see what has been hooked.

* * *

In most forms of intellectual activity, a great deal of purification and boiling down occurs. We are like Madame Curie, faced with piles of black bituminous substance which has to be boiled down to produce a tiny amount of useful material. In film-making there are ratios between what is 'shot' or filmed, and what is finally used. Normally the ratio is about 10:1. Often it is much higher. One television series I was involved in shot 400 hours of film for a six hour series. The same is true of our writing, a 'collecting' to 'publishing' ratio of 100:1 or so.

As we collect materials it is impossible, as with film making, to be certain as to what will be most useful and necessary for us. We collect on a broad front and find that what we thought rather peripheral becomes central, and vice versa. It is therefore important not to be too directed and narrow in our collecting and not to throw material away. Even if it is not used in the current project, it may come in useful later. I personally apply the same approach to most of the experiences and materials of my life.

Over the years I have accumulated books, films, photographs, papers, so that I have a large barn full of them. It may be a little obsessive, and is only possible because I have not moved house too often. But I now find that often for a new project I can go back over previously half-used or ignored materials and bring them into a new project. Of course I can only do this if it is reasonably organized and accessible. So from time to time I try to improve the storage and indexing systems to make it more visible. In doing so, I uncover buried ideas and data I had long forgotten about.

In terms of data, all of the above can be likened to garden plots. Each required quite a lot of effort to construct. Each garden contains innumerable fruits and riches, only a tiny part of which I can ever use. Everything has to be done in order to make a part accessible. Before getting at the deeper level or, or growing the good fruits, a huge context or infrastructure is needed. People often try to take short cuts. But constructing these worlds is both fascinating, if also laborious and based on special techniques.

Writing or any other form of introverted creative activity is a lonely business. It is very difficult to share the creative moment, though it does momentarily happen in things like conversations, seminars etc. Most of us are not only lonely, but inadequate, to face the task.

Major intellectual discoveries require team-work. Without his crew and the botanist Banks, the amazing discoveries of Captain Cook could not have been made. It is very seldom that a single mind can achieve the great heights. There are the Newton or Einstein figures, but they are very rare. The more normal case is Crick and Watson and Wilkes and Pauling and Rosalind Franklin, and others, combined.

At the simplest level, I have found that when I am writing or working in some other way it is essential to know that at least one, and preferably several, other people out there in the world care about what I produce. The 'ordeal by loneliness' which is a definition of Ph.D. research, applies to many other things. Yet it is not easy to work with others; pride, intellectual property rights, a divergence of interests and many other factors can easily interfere.

I have found it best to try to work with people intensively in a team for a limited period on a joint project where we can all contribute and also all benefit, and then to go our separate ways. With Sarah I have been involved in half a dozen of these projects, often based around computers and multi-media databases. Each one brought its satisfactions and then came to an end. The charismatic phase does not last for more than a few years, and it is easy to be trapped into routinization. It is far more satisfactory, if possible, to have a burst of creative collaboration, make something together, and then to part as friends.

* * *

There is an inevitable tendency for the mind to run in grooves, to find ourselves digging away deeper and deeper in the same mine shaft. The first digging has produced ore, a lot of infrastructure has been laid down. To go back up to the surface and try elsewhere is a huge effort, and a great risk. Even if, as almost always happens, the first seam becomes less productive, it is less stressful and feels safer to go on living off the diminishing returns from further working.

To change the metaphor to slash and burn agriculture, it is less effort to go on gardening in the same cleared forest patch, even if the returns rapidly diminish, than to abandon it and move on to the risky and hard labour of clearing huge trees for a new garden.

Yet most of the creative people I know constantly move on. If I had been more cautious and followed the usual course of academic life, I would have remained in the general field of early modern British social history, with special reference to 'anthropological' kinds of things – witches, sex, kinship, myth. A perfectly good career and reputation, and perhaps even distinctions and honours might have come my way if I had done so.

Instead I have shifted dramatically every few years. The location of the work has moved; England, Nepal, Japan and now China. The topics or subject has drifted here and there; witches, demography, individualism, crime, marriage, disease, political theory, technology, art, tea, education. Each was a new departure and sometimes required learning the basics of a new discipline.

The level and tone of the approach has varied. Sometimes it is heavily academic, with numerous quotations, masses of footnotes. More recently it is been more generally accessible, with quotes and notes at a minimum, short chapters, absence of jargon. I have also experimented with different forms of communication, books, articles, videodisc, databases, television series, websites.

The reason why this has worked for me is quite simple. The mind thrives on challenges, on freshness and change. Facts and landscapes very quickly become over familiar. The law of diminishing marginal returns always set in. We no longer notice things. The first creative energy comes from the burning of the primeval forest. A new array of 'facts' are consumed and puzzles and challenges abound. Then for a year or two there is a rich harvest of ideas and writing. But after two or three years (or when learning, as in a Ph.D., perhaps four years), the returns dramatically diminish. It is time to move on.

Changing the metaphor to that of a journey of exploration, Captain Cook or Darwin in the Beagle stayed for days, weeks, and sometimes months at a particularly interesting place, be it Hawaii or the Galapagos Islands. But then they moved on somewhere else. Opening up new mental frontiers is the exciting work. It is in this moment of the intersection between the known and the unknown that creativity occurs. Once the place or subject is understood, move on.

This is because most work is ultimately a matter of facing the mysterious and the unknown and trying to make sense of it. It is in those hours or days or months that the mind is trying to comprehend that we create. In a sense, a book or film is an attempt to explain to ourselves or others how things work. It is like doing a cross-word or jigsaw puzzle. The excitement is in solving the puzzle. Once it is done, it is over, dead, to be put up in a frame or returned to its box.

Few artists paint the same scene again and again, though Monet and his lily lake is a partial exception. So we should move on and be invigorated not just by slight, but by substantial changes.

* * *

If the whole process is like a journey, it is important to keep a journal of some kind, or at least to record the traces of the journey. Over time I have increasingly realized the importance of keeping a note of my travels. I do various things. I keep a sheet where I write in half a dozen words a day what I have done, or intend to do. Today I have written 'Writing to Rosa; Department – Chris; Foley Lecture.' This enables me quickly to see when I started and ended things, how long they took, what the shifting patterns of my work are.

I write our family diary at the week-ends, where I note any particular patterns to the week or any major changes or achievements in a few lines. I also have a 'Thoughts' book, which I have kept since 1978. Every few months at some turning point like the start or end of a period teaching or research, I write down a page or two of ideas of what I have been doing and plans for future work. It allows me to stand back, to look up into the blue skies and dream. Many of these ideas never come to anything, or lay dormant for many years.

I try to keep as full a record as possible of what I am currently working on. In the old days I kept the various typed drafts as they were made. Now the temptation is to throw away everything, both paper and computer earlier versions, so as not to take up too much space and not to clutter up our work space.

This may be necessary, but I like to keep the versions where there have been substantial changes and sometimes it makes a big difference. Sometimes a whole section that was earlier cut out of one work may become relevant again, some references that have been lost in the revisions can be restored, and I can go back to the originals.

Above all I like to keep the various outline plans of where a book is going. Placing them side by side often helps to jog the mind into fresh thought and to show where we veered off in an unproductive direction.

There is nowadays another reason for keeping the workings. The great student of mythology and language, Max Muller, published a book called 'Chips from a German Workshop.' These were the chips, or small pieces, cut off from his huge work on comparative mythologies. All of us produce chips which are not part of the major work, but may be useful to others. In the past these were lost. Nowadays they can be made available, as I have tried to do, on the web as separate appendices.

* * *

At the deepest level you probably need to think of why you are engaged on the adventure or journey at all. If it is for only one motive – money, fame, immortality, status, to solve puzzles, to understand your world, to have adventures with friends – it will probably not work. You will find that not enough of any of these things will come your way, except perhaps understanding. It is much better to have several, or even all, of these motives together. Then you will often find that while you are concentrating on one, another will partially be fulfilled.

This has certainly been my experience. I did not write my books on Witchcraft, Individualism or Glass in the belief that they would make money, though they did make some. Nor did I explicitly write them for fame or to promote my career, though they partially achieved bits of this. Most creative people enjoy the chase and the game, the 'mad pursuit' as Crick calls it. If there is a good meal to be had from what they have hunted down at the end, that is a bonus. But the fact that most people in England hunt inedible and useless things, coarse fish, foxes and so on, suggests that it is the pursuit which comes first.

Like all playful behaviour, which is what intellectual work is most like, the game is an end in itself. The mind dances and plays and we delight. If people clap us, or even put their hands in their pockets to make further performances possible, that is a bonus.

* * *

I have not talked about the role of chance, but obviously that is one of the main things. In my life I have had enormous good luck, to be born into relative affluence, to have had excellent teachers, to have had good friends, to have met and worked with Sarah, to have enjoyed the enormous support of Gerry, to worked with bright younger scholars over the years. To have met friends in Nepal and China. To have chanced on the Gurungs and met Dilmaya. To be in Cambridge and at King's College. To be living through a communications revolution.

The fact is that luck is cumulative as well. I often used to think of my life as like a salmon going up a river. If I was lucky enough to leap a waterfall at the first or second try, I could then rest and move swiftly forward. Yet I saw around me many people who were just as intelligent, talented and hard-working, if not more so, who grew exhausted as they tried to leap out of a certain pool. My conclusion was that if I put a huge burst of energy into leaping up the stream early in life, as I did, then it would pay off as one cleared the early waterfalls.

This was much easier to do in the fortunate period when I was your age. The world seemed much more open. Yet it may be that it is partly compensated for by changes in where the luck would lead us. I would probably, almost certainly, not have ended up as a British academic if I were eighteen today. I would probably have gone to University, but then travelled, and then, knowing what I know now, have settled somewhere in East Asia, perhaps China, where a whole new world is opening up.

So how do we spot and attract luck? All I can say is that one builds on the cumulative nature of good fortune. The luck of my parents and Oxford and Nepal, made the luck of Sarah possible. The luck of fascinating multi-media projects and Cambridge attracted the luck of Gerry. The luck of Gerry made my current work on digital and web systems with younger colleagues possible. Of course bad luck, illness, sadness, loss, can then throw it all down again. Yet hopefully, as success breeds success, as your work and interest and luck increases, it becomes like a tide or successful advancing army. There are delays, setbacks, slowness. Yet if the tide advances along a wide beach, these do not matter too much.

* * *

In all of this, returning to an earlier point, the beginnings are the most vulnerable. Most of us can make a project do interesting things once it is well under way. It is the early stages when all one has is a dream, a rather half-baked plan, that things are critically difficult. In my early days I had plenty of these dreams, and Sarah, who is logical, cautious, an avoider of undue risks, was always sceptical and often quite critical. I suppose that now, as she says (and this is another way of putting the idea of success breeding success), she is more likely to trust these wild schemes. She has seen that however mad they sound, they often work.

This is an important development. Most artists and scientists are backed at first for their potential, their form and experience, as much as for their particular current plan or project. A rough knowledge of their previous achievements is built into the assessment of their backers. It takes time to build up the portfolio of successes and experience. So, at the start, you are mostly alone. The only person who really knows what you are capable of and believes in you is you yourself. If you do not project quiet self-confidence, then why should anyone trust you?

Of course this is not easy. Often you set off without knowing that you can succeed. You lead a band of followers with the inner knowledge that it is the blind leading the blind. This is bound to be the case. If you look at the diaries of many great men they are constantly assailed with doubts and think of themselves as shallow and unworthy.

In a sense this is the world of the Hobbits or Harry Potter. The essence of those books is the knowledge that the task is almost impossible. Yet it must be attempted and, against all the odds, achieved. I have often thought, and often been told, that my major asset is dogged self-confidence. For whatever reason, I have always believed that almost anybody can do (almost) anything if they really want to – which Einstein on a number of occasions endorsed, saying he was not of above average ability etc.

Just as Roosevelt pointed out that 'all we have to fear is fear itself', we might say that 'all we have to doubt is doubt itself.' Believe in yourself, try, and often you'll succeed beyond your wildest drams. One begins to understand those old school and University mottos. Mine at preparatory school, when translated from latin, was 'By hard work to the stars.' That in Hokkaido University in Japan is 'Boys be ambitious.'

ALAN MACFARLANE

How we Understand the World

THIS BOOK IS part of a series of short letters written to young friends. Encouraged by the reception of my *Letters to Lily* (2005), I decided to write a set of letters to her younger sister—*Reflections for Rosa*. I was then asked by other friends to write short books for their children.

In each I try to explore some aspect of 'How we Understand the World', based on my experience as an anthropologist and historian at Cambridge University. I have tried to put into simple words what I have learnt about discovery, creativity and methods to understand our complex world.

EXPLORE THE SERIES

CAM RIVERS
PUBLISHING

Image on front cover is an adaptation of Armed Three-master with Daedalus and Icarus in the Sky from The Sailing Vessels, courtesy of the Metropolitan Museum of Art, Harris Brisbane Dick Fund, 1928, available under the Creative Commons CC0 1.0 Universal Public Domain Dedication.

29167739R00055

Printed in Great Britain
by Amazon